LOST
IN THE
MUSEUM

WRITTEN BY **WILL MABBITT**   ILLUSTRATED BY **AARON CUSHLEY**

INTRODUCTION

Seven-year-old Stevie is lost in The Metropolitan Museum of Art! Can you help her find her way out and back to her family?

As Stevie moves through the museum's different galleries there are many exciting things for her to see and find. Her brother Alfie has left her a trail of items to guide her on her way. But there are also clues to watch out for among the fascinating museum artworks—and some surprising extra things, too!

See the museum through Stevie's eyes as she embarks on an imaginative voyage of discovery. Travel with her all over the world and from the ancient past to the present day. Then at the back of the book learn more about what Stevie saw on her adventure and the items you too can find in The Metropolitan Museum of Art—and turn back to the beginning to see what you missed!

Look out for recurring characters, too. See if you can spot some of these people along the way ...

LOOK OUT FOR PROMPTS LIKE THIS ONE—AND SEE WHAT YOU CAN SEEK AND FIND ON EVERY PAGE!

Stevie's mom

Stevie

Alfie (Stevie's brother)

Pigeon

Professor Annabel (museum curator)

Mr. Pebbles (janitor)

Gloves

CAN YOU FIND ALL THE MISSING ITEMS?

Sneakers

Lunch box

Mr. Ted

Bottle

Socks

Scarf

Squeaky toy

Coat

Hat

Alfie's drawing

Teapot

Blanket

Jeffrey (security guard)

Sushma (security guard)

Gladys

Crispin

Corina

Zac

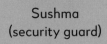

Stevie was lost in the museum. One minute she and Mom had been looking at a beaked griffin— a mythical creature, part eagle, part lion, cast from bronze—and the next she was all alone with the Greek and Roman statues.

She repeated the instructions Mom had given her in case they became separated: "Head to the Great Hall, and I'll meet you there."

It sounded simple, but the museum was huge and full of people and ... things. Where was the Great Hall, and—wait, Stevie spotted something! It was her brother Alfie's blue hat! Alfie was always losing things. Maybe he'd left a trail of belongings that could lead her to the Great Hall ...

WHERE IS THE GRIFFIN? WHAT OTHER CREATURES CAN YOU SEE?

WHAT HAS
SUSHMA THE
SECURITY GUARD
FOUND?

Suddenly, Stevie was very high up, at the top
of the museum. New York City stretched
into the distance. Stevie felt very small.

A red-tailed hawk swooped past. Stevie followed
its flight over the Roof Garden. She imagined
having eyes like a hawk and looked around
for something that Alfie might have dropped.
She could see sculptures, plants, children—
and one of Alfie's sneakers!

Stevie's Mom and brother had definitely
been this way. She wondered what
treasures the next room would hold ...

CAN YOU
SPOT THE
RED-TAILED
HAWK?

Stevie blinked. This room sparkled—shiny weapons and armor were everywhere! One suit of armor had been a gift to a five-year-old child—Infante Luis, Prince of Asturias. "Alfie would love a present like that," Stevie muttered.

"Alfie?" said a jolly voice. "Was that the young man who lost his glove? Easily done!" Stevie span around, but no one was there. Just an empty suit of armor belonging to George Clifford, the Third Earl of Cumberland.

"Imagine paddling in one of those!" said Stevie to herself, in a room full of art from Africa, Oceania, and the Americas. She was standing next to a carved Asmat canoe from southwest New Guinea. Somehow it made her feel better about being lost in the museum. She imagined she was an explorer lost at sea, except then she might have navigational charts to guide the way and all she had was her little brother's glove!

But wait! There was Alfie's other sneaker—showing her the way to go.

LOOK OUT FOR FIVE PATTERNED FABRIC TUNICS AND WRAPPERS.

HOW MANY
MASKS CAN YOU FIND?
WHAT EXPRESSIONS
ARE THEY MAKING?

15

Following her nose, Stevie found herself in the restaurant.
It was very busy and Stevie was very hungry. She gazed
at the doughnuts sadly. They looked and smelled delicious!
If she and Alfie had been good, Mom might have bought
them one. Everyone seemed happy with their food—apart
from a little bear sitting on his own. "Oh no!" cried Stevie.
"That's no ordinary bear. That's Alfie's Mr. Ted!"
If Alfie noticed Mr. Ted was gone, there would be
tears. Stevie needed to find him, fast.

CAN YOU FIND
THE PIGEON?

16

WHICH ITEMS FROM THIS STORAGE ROOM WOULD YOU DISPLAY IN YOUR MUSEUM?

Stevie's eyes opened wide.
It would be very difficult to find a teapot among all these other objects.
Luckily for the curator, Stevie had lots of practice finding things in the museum.
The curator was very pleased to have Stevie's help, but there was no sign
that Mom or Alfie had been this way ...

In the Asian Art gallery, Stevie was approached by a girl looking for a statue of Ganesha. Stevie knew about Ganesha, the elephant-headed Hindu god. She'd learned about him in school!

Apparently, Ganesha was the remover of obstacles. Stevie needed help with the obstacles on her path through the museum. "Maybe there's a clue in the next room," she wondered aloud. Stevie couldn't be sure, but it looked like Ganesha nodded!

LOOK OUT FOR ONE RABBIT, ONE STAG, ONE RHINO, AND TWO LIONS!

THE ELEPHANT STATUE GANESHA IS DANCING. CAN YOU FIND ANY OTHER STATUES THAT LOOK LIKE THEY ARE DANCING?

21

The next archway led to a room full of European sculptures. Stevie stopped at the statue of ancient Greek hero Perseus holding the head of the Gorgon Medusa. "If I could borrow your winged sandals, then I could fly up high for a better look!" she said. The head of the mythical Gorgon seemed to be looking at something. When Stevie followed its stony gaze, she saw ...

... Alfie's bottle! Stevie was back on the trail. She knew she needed to keep searching for more clues. She thanked the Gorgon before moving on.

CAN YOU SEE THE ARTWORK OF A GARDEN SCENE? A LADY IS RESTING WITH A DRINK AND TWO OTHERS ARE SERVING FRUIT.

In the next room, Stevie tripped and fell over another visitor!

From the floor she looked around the room of Islamic Art in wonder. These were the biggest carpets she'd ever seen. It wasn't just the rugs that were grand. Everywhere she looked were beautiful textiles, detailed paintings ... and a blue sock?

As Stevie got up, she had a funny feeling she might have forgotten something.

HOW MANY HORSES CAN YOU FIND ON THESE ARTWORKS? WHERE IS THE ELEPHANT?

25

The next room was like a fashion show through time, it was so full of clothes. There were dresses and suits of all sorts—from 19th-century French wedding dresses to woolen bathing suits from New York. And shoes, so many shoes!

LOOK FOR THE WHITE, RUFFLED WEDDING DRESS FROM FRANCE FROM 1864.

All of the clothes were beautifully presented—apart from one. A single sock lay crumpled on the floor. It wasn't part of a display, it belonged to Alfie!

Shh! Stevie had wandered into a large auditorium. The curator she'd met earlier was standing on the stage giving a talk about teapots.

Mom and Alfie must have wandered through here, too, because there was Alfie's lunchbox! Stevie doubted they would have stayed very long. Alfie wasn't good at staying quiet!

And without his snacks, Alfie must be hungry ... There was no time to lose!

WHAT SORT OF OBJECT FROM THE MUSEUM WOULD YOU LIKE TO GIVE A TALK ABOUT?

Stevie loved painting. In the European Paintings hall she paused by the artwork named *Blind Orion Searching for the Rising Sun* by Nicolas Poussin.

Orion must have been a giant, because he seemed as tall as a tree. Like Stevie, Orion was looking for something.

Stevie stood on tiptoes—as tall as Orion—to get a better view of the room. Around a corner, there was Alfie's purple blanket!

The next room was filled with modern and contemporary art from the last 100 years. Stevie peered at a painting by Jackson Pollock. It was all splattery. Stevie thought it was great. "I bet that was fun to do!" she said.

A museum janitor walked past. "I wouldn't have wanted to clean up afterward, though," he grumbled. Stevie laughed. She imagined what Mom would say if she started splattering paint around like that when she was painting at home. It would be worth it if the picture ended up in a museum!

Then Stevie noticed an artwork on the floor. Instead of oil or acrylic paints, this was done with crayon scribbles. It was by Alfie. He must have been this way!

It couldn't be as big as these beasts—they would never fit in her apartment! Just then she noticed something out of place …

Past a bull and a frog, was Alfie's zebra-striped coat! Alfie had dropped so much stuff Stevie was running out of space in her bag. The sooner she could hand it all back the better!

WHICH ARTIFACT IS DECORATED WITH A MOUNTAIN GOAT?

The next room was full of musical instruments from around the world! There were instruments that Stevie recognized, and some that didn't look like anything she'd seen before!

LOOK FOR ALL THE INSTRUMENTS THAT USE STRINGS, LIKE THE VIOLINS.

THE ORGAN IS
THE BIGGEST INSTRUMENT
IN THE MUSEUM. WHICH
IS THE SMALLEST YOU
CAN FIND?

Stevie was in a band at school.
It would be cool to play the Indian Taūs,
shaped like a peacock. Speaking of music,
what was that familiar—annoying—tune?

It sounded like the musical parrot that was
usually strapped to Alfie's stroller. Mom, Alfie,
and the Great Hall couldn't be far away!

Stevie's confidence changed to confusion as, in the American Wing, she thought she had left the museum and was back outside on the street! Then she realized that the grand building in front of her was an old bank—the American Bank—that had been moved, marble stone by stone, inside the museum.

If the museum could get one giant building to fit inside another, then nothing was impossible. Stevie looked around and spotted something familiar—Alfie's striped scarf!

WHAT COLORS AND SHAPES ARE USED IN THE TIFFANY STAINED-GLASS WINDOW?

Stevie gasped as the Egyptian Temple of Dendur loomed before her. It was as if she really was in ancient Egypt, on the banks of the Nile River. In ancient times people would have traveled from far and wide to see the temple, just as they travel from all over the world to visit the museum. Stevie frowned as she saw a flash of purple in the distance ... It was Mom and Alfie!

Stevie rubbed her eyes and, just like that, Mom and Alfie had disappeared. Where had they gone?

MANY EGYPTIAN OBJECTS WERE MADE FROM A BLUE CERAMIC CALLED FAIENCE. HOW MANY CAN YOU SPOT?

EGYPTIANS BELIEVED THAT SOME FIGURES COULD MAGICALLY COME ALIVE! CAN YOU FIND A SMALL BLUE-GREEN CERAMIC HIPPO?

41

There was an eerie silence. Standing before Stevie and the door that Mom must have passed through was the Tomb of Perneb! To follow Mom, Stevie would have to enter the tomb! She shuddered.

When the tomb was built in ancient Egypt, Perneb would have been buried deep below, his internal organs stored in jars next to his stone sarcophagus. Stevie imagined what that would have been like and hoped he wouldn't mind her passing through without bringing a lavish offering.

Another visitor had left something, though ... It was Alfie's other glove! Taking a deep breath, Stevie stepped into the tomb to claim it back.

A gift shop! Stevie had learned a lot of new things at the museum, but if there was one subject she was already an expert in, it was gift shops! They were always next to the way in and the way out in museums.

Normally, Stevie would have liked to spend some time looking though all the souvenirs, but she was too excited to get to the Great Hall where she knew Mom and Alfie would be waiting.

WHICH ITEMS
DO YOU RECOGNIZE
FROM THE MUSEUM?

On the other side of the shop, beyond the
pencils, pens, postcards, and toys, Stevie could
see a sign pointing to the Great Hall!

In the Great Hall, Stevie ran straight into the arms
of Mom and Alfie! Stevie was pleased to see Mom,
but not as pleased as Mom was to see her.

She picked Stevie up and gave her the biggest
hug ever. Alfie grinned, too. Stevie reached into
her bag to get Mr. Ted. But Mr. Ted was gone!
"I must have dropped him!" Stevie spluttered.
"Dropped who?" asked Mom.
"Mr. Ted!" said Alfie, pointing at Mr. Ted.
Somehow, Mr. Ted had found his way back, too.

"Well done, Stevie!" said Mom. "I knew you would
remember what I said. But I'm afraid it's time to go
home. I'm sorry we didn't get to see much in the
museum. We'll come back again another day."
Stevie just smiled. "I can't wait!" she said.

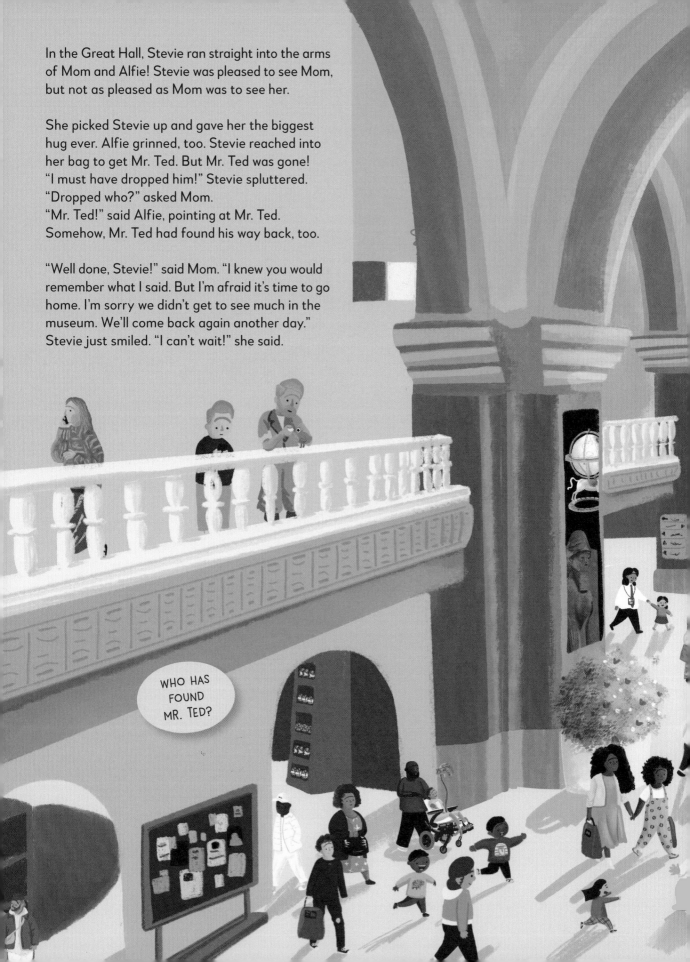

GREEK AND R☮MAN ART

Stevie starts her adventure looking for her mom and brother, but she discovers so much more along the way! The first room she explores, on pages 8–9, contains classical art and sculpture from ancient civilizations Greece and Rome.

This marble statue shows the Three Graces, who appear in Greek and Roman mythology. The Graces were called Beauty, Mirth, and Abundance, but it is hard to tell which is which without their heads! Can you draw a different face for each of the Graces? Perhaps Mirth is laughing!

The Three Graces, 2nd century CE, Roman

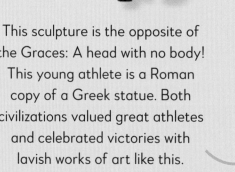

Ancient statues are often missing parts. Usually it's just because the statue is very old.

This sculpture is the opposite of the Graces: A head with no body! This young athlete is a Roman copy of a Greek statue. Both civilizations valued great athletes and celebrated victories with lavish works of art like this.

Head of an Athlete, c. 138–192 CE, Roman

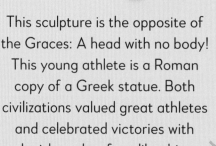

Terracotta Panathenaic Prize Amphora, c. 530 BCE, Greek

This amphora was a prize in a Greek sporting event held to honor the goddess Athena. One decorated side shows the event and the other shows Athena. It would have been filled with olive oil before being presented to the victor. Events like these inspired the modern Olympic Games!

This life-size lion statue would have been used to guard a tomb, so it needed to look intimidating. Lions didn't live in Greece when this statue was made, but they are an important part of Greek art and mythology. The sculptor might have based the sculpture on a dog instead!

Marble Statue of a Lion,
c. 400–390 BCE, Greek

Can you find this small bronze statue of a horse in the Greek and Roman gallery? It isn't life-size, in fact it isn't even 7 inches (18 cm) tall! This bronze horse has a geometric design, which isn't as realistic as the lion, but suggests the form of a horse in simple, elegant shapes.

What other statues can you find in the gallery?

Bronze Horse,
8th century BCE, Greek

Bronze Chariot,
6th century BCE,
Etruscan

This chariot is Etruscan, belonging to a civilization that lived in Italy before the Romans. The chariot would have been pulled by two horses and used in parades to carry a very important person. It is decorated with images of Achilles, the Greek hero of the Trojan War. In the front panel, he is being given armor by his mother.

ARMS AND ARMOR

Do you remember the Third Earl of Cumberland from the Arms and Armor room on pages 12–13? Some of the suits of armor standing alongside him are from the medieval or Renaissance eras, or even later, and from places such as Germany, Italy, and Japan. Take a look at the different styles!

George Clifford, the Third Earl of Cumberland, was one of Queen Elizabeth I's favorite knights. If you look very closely at the details right in the middle of his chestplate you might be able to spot the letter E—a tribute to the Queen.

This armor was used for jousting. It also has Tudor rose and French fleur-de-lis decorations.

Armor for Man and Horse, dated 1548, with later restorations, Kunz Lochner, German

Armor of George Clifford (1558–1605), Third Earl of Cumberland, dated 1586, Britain

Stevie thinks it must have been hard work putting on a suit of armor—and even harder getting onto a horse while wearing it. Did you find all four German knights mounted on their shiny steeds? This armor may have been made for a very special ceremony in Germany in 1548.

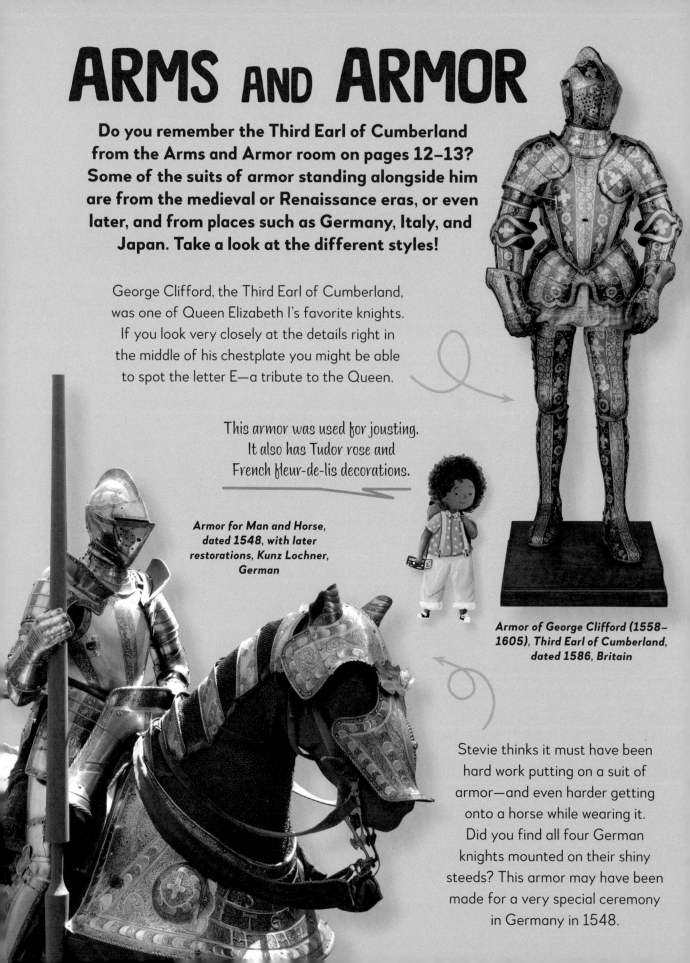

This visored Italian helmet has a special name—burgonet—and has a decorative mermaid crest. The mermaid is holding something in her hands—the head of a lady with snakes for hair. Stevie recognizes the head from the European Sculpture hall. Can you find her there? It is the Gorgon known as Medusa.

Burgonet, dated 1543, Filippo Negroli, Italian

What symbols would you like on your coat of arms?

This Japanese mask would have been worn to protect a soldier's face in combat. It has a silk lining to make it more comfortable to wear. Stevie thinks that the angry mask would have made the wearer even more intimidating than they already were! Can you make a similar, battle-ready expression?

There's a special, colorful, Japanese piece of armor in the gallery—called a Gusoku. Can you find it?

Mask, dated 1745, inscribed by Myōchin Muneakira, Japanese

ARTS of AFRICA, OCEANIA, AND THE AMERICAS

The art in this gallery comes from all over the globe. Some of it is well over 1,000 years old, while some was created as recently as the past century. Stevie was fascinated to discover more about the different objects and the cultures they come from.

This large volcanic rock has been carved to show a snarling, pouncing jaguar! Jaguars are one of the biggest predators in the Americas. The first thing you notice are the jaguar's deep, sunken eyes. The eye sockets might have once contained polished obsidian to give the big cat shining eyes. Can you also identify its pointy fangs, rough tongue, flattened ears, and curved claws?

Feline Sculpture, 7th–10th century, Veracruz

Stevie discovered that this Inca tapestry tunic was made from camelid hair. Camelid describes any animal from the camel family. In South America, that includes llamas, alpacas, guanacos, and vicuñas. Cloth was very important in Inca culture. It was often given as a gift, exchanged, or ceremonially burned to mark special occasions.

Checkerboard Tunic, 16th century, Inca

What other fabrics can you find in this room? Take a look on pages 14–15!

This tall, oval shape was common in Solomon Islanders' shields from this period. However, this shield is painted and decorated with tiny pieces of shimmering shell, which isn't very common! War shields would have normally just been made of woven wicker, so it is likely this one was only used for ceremonies or as a symbol of high status.

Memorial Heads (Ntiri),
c. 17th century, Akan peoples, Ghana

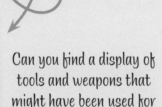

Can you find a display of tools and weapons that might have been used for more practical purposes?

The Akan peoples include many smaller groups who share elements of their language and culture. For many centuries, Akan women potters made terracotta sculptures such as these, in memory of the dead. Sculptures vary a lot in design—they can be round or flat, hollow or solid.

Shield (Grere'o),
early 19th century,
Solomon Islands

This mask is made from lots of natural materials, including turtle shell, feathers, twine, and wood. It comes from the Torres Strait Islands, between Australia and New Guinea. It may have been worn by a dancer retelling the story of a legendary hero. The hero must have had a special link with the bird depicted above the head.

Mask
(Buk, Krar, or Kara),
mid- to late 19th
century, Torres
Strait Islands

ASIAN ART

In the Asian Art gallery on pages 20–21, Stevie helps an artist find an Indian statue of Ganesha. The room also holds objects from many other countries, including China, Japan, and Korea.

Can you believe that this jar is over 600 years old? Stevie wondered how it could have survived so long without breaking! The vase shows a majestic dragon flying through a cloudy sky. The blue-and-white color combination is common in Chinese ceramics from this time.

Jar with Dragon, early 15th century, China

Under the Wave off Kanagawa (Kanagawa oki nami ura), also known as The Great Wave c. 1830–1832, Katsushika Hokusai, Japanese

If you look closely, one of the white-topped peaks in this picture isn't a wave—it is a mountain! Even Mount Fuji, Japan's highest mountain, looks small compared to this mighty crashing wave. Made using a woodblock printing technique, this famous scene has inspired many copies. Why not make your own version?

This is my favorite picture in this room. What is yours?

This bronze dragon still has a gleam in its eye, even though it is over 1,000 years old! Originally, this lucky creature would have been attached to the corner of a roof on a grand building or temple. It may not be able to roar, but the loop below its mouth used to hold a bell, making it a wind chime!

Dragon's Head Rafter Finial 10th century, Korea

Chamunda, the Horrific Destroyer of Evil 10th–11th century, India

Chamunda is a fierce form of the Hindu goddess Kali and is associated with disease and decay. She uses her power to destroy evil. Her arms are broken here, but once there would have been 12! Despite the damage, there are still lots of details to discover—skulls on her headdress, a snake as a necklace, and a scorpion on her stomach.

Did you see one of the smallest items in the gallery? This ivory rabbit is only 1 inch (2.5 cm) tall, so might be hard to spot! This tiny sculpture is a Japanese netsuke. It was worn at the end of a cord to hold a small purse or container on someone's clothing.

This was displayed next to a stag-shaped belt pendant. Can you find both?

Netsuke of Rabbit, 19th century, Japan

EUROPEAN SCULPTURE

Stevie met mythical Gorgon Medusa in this gallery, on pages 22–23. Medusa could apparently turn people to stone by looking at them. There are some statues here, but there are also artifacts made of marble, porcelain, bronze, and more.

This globe maps the stars. It used to rotate and was displayed in a curiosity cabinet belonging to Holy Roman Emperor Rudolf II. Stevie could see constellations she recognized from staring at the night sky. Even the winged horse beneath is a reference to a constellation—Pegasus.

Celestial globe with clockwork, 1579 Gerhard Emmoser, Austrian

What do you think he is thinking about?

This sculpture of a ballerina was originally made in wax. She wears a real tutu and hair ribbon! After the artist, Degas, died, the sculpture was cast in bronze many times over so it could be preserved, sold, and exhibited across the world. Can you stand in the same ballet pose?

The Little Fourteen-Year-Old Dancer, 1922 (cast), 2018 (tutu), Edgar Degas, French

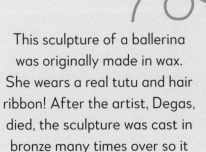

The Thinker, modeled c. 1880, cast c. 1910, Auguste Rodin, French

Did you notice this ewer? Most jugs like this would have been used for carrying water. But this one was made in a workshop that produced luxury goods for a very important family in Florence, Italy— the Medici.

This bronze statue by Rodin is called *The Thinker*. Stevie thinks he looks like he is thinking about something very serious. Some people believe he is thinking about life and death. He was originally made to sit over a huge, sculpted doorway.

Ewer (Brocca), c. 1575–1587 Medici Porcelain Manufactory, Italian

EUROPEAN PAINTINGS

The European Paintings gallery displays some artworks Stevie knew and some she didn't. Which are your favorite pieces from pages 30–31? Where in Europe are they from? See if you can find out!

Irises, 1890, Vincent van Gogh, Dutch

Stevie found this oil painting by Dutch artist Vincent van Gogh calming. In fact, this was the intention—Vincent van Gogh believed the violet flowers against the pink background created a "harmonious" effect. Do any other paintings change how you are feeling? What colors do the artists use?

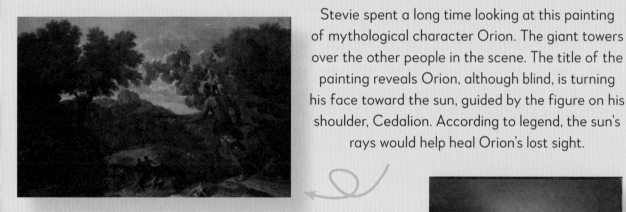

Stevie spent a long time looking at this painting of mythological character Orion. The giant towers over the other people in the scene. The title of the painting reveals Orion, although blind, is turning his face toward the sun, guided by the figure on his shoulder, Cedalion. According to legend, the sun's rays would help heal Orion's lost sight.

Blind Orion Searching for the Rising Sun, 1658, Nicolas Poussin, French

Do you know any other paintings by Vincent van Gogh?

Spanish artist Goya painted this artwork of young Manuel, the son of the Count and Countess of Altamira, in a bright red outfit. Stevie liked the details at the boy's feet. Can you see the cats staring at the magpie and the cage of finches?

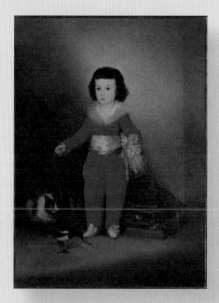

Manuel Osorio Manrique de Zuñiga (1787–1788), Francisco Goya, Spanish

ISLAMIC ART

Stevie dropped Mr. Ted in this room, but picked up some interesting facts about Islamic art. Some of the carpets in this gallery originally decorated the floors of palaces. There are also tiled wall panels, pages from illustrated books, vases, and metal sculptures to be found.

Unlike Stevie, elephants never forget, but do you remember this painting from the gallery? It is titled *Three Noblemen in Procession on an Elephant*. Can you see the three noblemen? They are wearing gold and pearl necklaces. Indian soldiers lead the way at the front of the procession.

Three Noblemen in Procession on an Elephant c. 1790, Venkatchellum, Indian

How many people do you suppose have walked on this carpet through the ages?

Speaking of animals, Stevie thought this silk animal rug was beautiful. It displays very fine, intricate work. Look closely and the details might surprise you. Lions, tigers, rams, deer, and even dragons are locked in deadly combat!

Silk Animal Carpet, 16th century, Iran

Do you like this painting of a blue horse and a boy? The runner is a groom, someone who takes care of horses. The royal horse carries an elaborate saddle. The piece has been painted using bright inks, including gold.

Royal Horse and Runner, 16th–17th century, India

Incense Burner of Amir Saif al-Dunya wa'l-Din ibn Muhammad al-Mawardi, 1181–1182 CE, Ja`far ibn Muhammad ibn `Ali, found in Iran

This lion would have lived in a palace!

Incense burners were used to perfume the air with scented smoke. Animal-shaped examples like this lion-horse hybrid were common. This feline is exceptional due to its size—it is 34 inches (86 cm) tall and 33 inches (83 cm) long! Incense was inserted by removing its head, then scented smoke would have escaped from the small holes in its body.

There are other items with writing on them in the Islamic Art gallery on pages 24–25. Can you find them?

Can you find this turquoise jug in the gallery? It's decorated with mythical harpies and sphinxes. Harpies are birds with human faces and sphinxes are lions with human heads. There's a secret message written around the rim and at the base—two love poems, one by a known Persian poet and the other by an unknown author.

Pierced Jug with Harpies and Sphinxes, 1215–1216 CE, Iran

THE COSTUME INSTITUTE

This gallery seemed very crowded, until Stevie realized that some of the figures were exhibits! What similarities can you identify between what we wear today and clothes from centuries ago?

Court dress, c. 1750, Great Britain

This huge skirt would have been held out by an undergarment known as a hoop, which was usually made of whalebone or cane. The person wearing it would have had to walk through doors sideways! Although this dress is British, the style is influenced by French court fashion.

This tiny parasol wouldn't be much use in the rain! It was designed to keep the sun off the owner's face and was bought for a young girl named Juliette by her Aunt Julia. There is another parasol in the costume gallery—can you find it?

Parasol, 1886, United States

Which item in the gallery would you like to wear, and why? Turn to pages 26–27!

This French cape is made from expensive silk velvet from China, woven with gilt threads. Many of the clothes in the Costume gallery once belonged to very wealthy people. Why do you think clothes worn by ordinary people might not have been preserved?

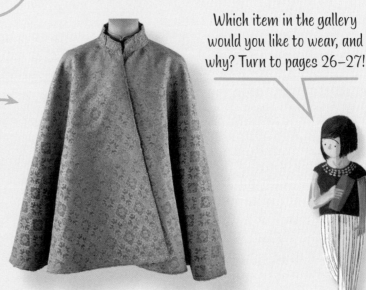

Cape, 16th century, France

MUSICAL INSTRUMENTS

Music is a language shared by everyone. This room contains instruments from all around the world. Look back at pages 36–37. Which would you most like to hear played?

The violin in the Musical Instruments gallery was made by Antonio Stradivari. Today, his violins are treasured by musicians and collectors, but they are very rare. They can be worth millions of dollars.

"The Antonius" Violin 1711, Antonio Stradivari, Italian

The reverse of the pipa is covered with more than 100 carved hexagons, decorated with symbols of happiness and good fortune. In the gallery, it is displayed with the back facing outward. Can you find it? Look for the pear-shaped body and four tuning pegs on the neck.

Pipa, late 16th–early 17th century, China

Japanese gongs from this period would usually have been used at tea ceremonies, in theaters, and in religious ceremonies. However, this gong held by two carved demons was mainly for display, even before it came to the museum!

Gong Held by Oni early 19th century, Japan

Can you find other percussion instruments in the gallery, such as drums?

Taūs (mayuri), 19th century, India

This stringed instrument shares some features with the lute, sarangi, and the sitar, but not its unusual peacock shape and design! It is even made with real peacock feathers. The peacock is associated with Sarasvatî, the Hindu goddess of music.

MODERN AND CONTEMPORARY ART

The Modern and Contemporary Art gallery displays more recent works of art from the last hundred years or so. The styles are more varied, sometimes abstract, or experimental. How do the pieces on pages 32–33 make you feel?

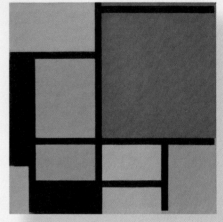

*Composition, 1921,
Piet Mondrian,
Dutch*

*Movement of Vaulted Chambers, 1915
Paul Klee, German, born Switzerland*

Dutch painter Piet Mondrian described this way of painting with geometric shapes "Neo-Plasticism." Can you count all 11 rectangles, all separated by thick black lines? Mondrian liked using primary colors—as seen here, with his use of red and blue.

Paul Klee, the artist behind this colorful painting, was inspired by music (having trained as a violinist), shapes, color, and modern-art movements of the time, seeking harmony in all he did. He produced more than 9,000 works of art in his lifetime!

What colors do you notice in the Modern Art room?

Artist Georgia O'Keeffe gathered sun-bleached bones from the New Mexico desert for paintings like this one. She liked the contrast of the white bones against the blue sky and examined all the details up close. She thought these bones were beautiful. What do you think?

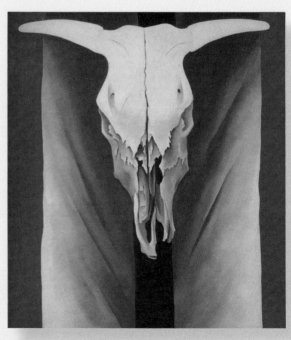

*Cow's Skull: Red, White, and Blue, 1931,
Georgia O'Keeffe, American*

THE AMERICAN WING

When Stevie first saw the Branch Bank she thought she was outside—but she was actually inside the museum's American Wing! This area, on pages 38–39, displays art from across American history.

This bank used to stand on Wall Street, New York. This wing of the museum was built around it. You can even walk through the door. If you could save a building and keep it safe in a museum forever, which would you choose?

I'd choose my local tea shop!

American Bank Branch Façade, 1822–1824, Martin E. Thompson, American

Diana, 1892–1893, cast 1928, Augustus Saint-Gaudens, American

Did you notice the golden statue of the Roman goddess Diana? Stevie discovered it was a smaller replica of a weather vane that was made for Madison Square Garden Tower in New York. The original one was too big. Can you see any weather vanes in your neighborhood? They are designed to turn and show which way the wind is blowing.

Bust of Hiawatha 1868, Edmonia Lewis, American

What is your favorite poem?

This bust is of Hiawatha from Henry Wadsworth Longfellow's epic poem, *The Song of Hiawatha*, written in 1855. The poem tells of a tragic romance between Hiawatha and Minnehaha, his starcrossed lover from a rival tribe. The artist, Edmonia Lewis, made several sculptures based on this poem.

ANCIENT NEAR EASTERN ART

The Ancient Near Eastern Art gallery is home to art from early civilizations in the Middle East. Look back at pages 34–35. This gallery contains some of the oldest objects in the museum—created 1,500–10,000 years ago!

Dress Ornament, c. 5th century BCE, possibly Russia

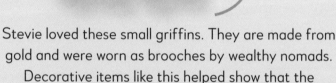

These griffins have catlike bodies and birds' wings. But griffins can be other combinations of animals, too.

Stevie loved these small griffins. They are made from gold and were worn as brooches by wealthy nomads. Decorative items like this helped show that the wearers were very powerful and important.

This horn is a drinking vessel called a rhyton. It is made from silver, so was probably used at royal parties. At one end is a panther. Examine its chest closely and you might be able to spot the spout for drinking out of! You might also notice decorations in the shape of grapes. These show that the horn was intended to hold wine.

Watch out for the claws!

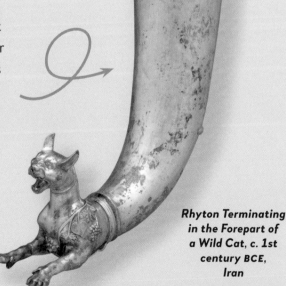

Rhyton Terminating in the Forepart of a Wild Cat, c. 1st century BCE, Iran

Did you find this frog in the gallery? It used to belong to a man named Iddin-Nergal. We know this because his name is written on the base. It was used as weight, to help measure how heavy things were.

Weight in the Shape of a Frog,
c. 2000–1600 BCE,
Iraq

The frog is like an early set of scales!

There are lots of horned animals in the Ancient Near Eastern Art rooms. Look for the oldest item in this book—it is the jar with the mountain goats painted on it.

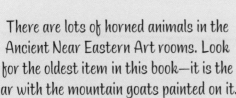

I think he was a good ruler.

Who is this ruler? Nobody knows for sure! The life-size head is made from copper alloy, which was a very expensive material, so he must have been a very important person. It's possible that the eyes, now empty spaces, once held different materials. Lots of detail has been added to his beard and mustache.

Head of a Ruler,
c. 2300–2000 BCE,
Iran or Iraq

I think he was mean!

EGYPTIAN ART

In the Egyptian Art galleries on pages 40–43, Stevie was stunned by the Temple of Dendur and the Tomb of Perneb. She found many items from ancient Egypt fascinating, from the smallest objects to the biggest ones ...

Did you notice this statue of Thoth, the ancient Egyptian god of writing, accounting, and all things intellectual? He was associated with two animals: an ibis (a type of bird) and a baboon. This statue shows Thoth as a human with an ibis head. There is also a statue of Thoth in baboon form. Can you find it?

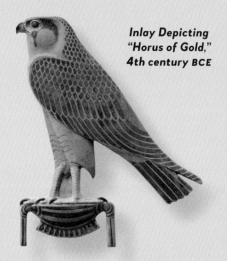

Inlay Depicting "Horus of Gold," 4th century BCE

Can you find any other hieroglyphs in the gallery?

Striding Thoth, 332–30 BCE

This is Horus, the ancient Egyptian falcon god of kingship. You might be able to find another example of Horus in the Egyptian Art gallery. This version of Horus is standing on a gold collar and is a hieroglyph—one of the special symbols used for writing in ancient Egypt. This symbol was used when writing royal names.

Stevie thought this ceramic hippo looked cute, but she knew that hippos could be very dangerous—and the ancient Egyptians knew this, too. This hippo was taken from the tomb of Senbi II along with a canopic box—used to store the internal organs of the dead. Nicknamed "William," this hippo may be small, but he is very special!

Hippopotamus ("William"), c. 1961–1878 BCE

*Seated Statue
of Hatshepsut*
c. 1479–1458 BCE

This limestone figure is Hatshepsut, one of the most
successful of several female rulers of ancient Egypt.
She has been sculpted life-size, sitting on her throne,
wearing her headcloth and her kilt—traditionally
clothing for a king. The hieroglyphs on her throne
are difficult to see but spell out her kingly title:
"The Perfect Goddess, Lady of the Two Lands."
What would you like your royal title to be?

In Greek mythology,
sphinxes like to ask
riddles. Do you know
any riddles?

This statue is also
Hatshepsut! Can you spot the
differences? Here she is shown as a collosal granite
sphinx—a creature with a lion's body, with her human head
and false beard. Long ago this statue would have guarded
Hatshepsut's mortuary temple alongside other sphinxes.

Sphinx of Hatshepsut
c. 1479–1458 BCE

Penguin Random House

Senior Editor Emma Grange
Senior Designer Anna Formanek
Project Editor Beth Davies
Designer Zoë Tucker
Picture Researchers Martin Copeland,
Sumedha Chopra, and Sumita Khatwani
Production Editor Siu Yin Chan
Senior Production Controller Lloyd Robertson
Managing Editor Paula Regan
Managing Art Editor Jo Connor
Publishing Director Mark Searle

First American Edition, 2021
Published in the United States by DK Publishing
1450 Broadway, Suite 801, New York, NY 10018

Page design copyright © 2021 Dorling Kindersley Limited
DK, a Division of Penguin Random House LLC
22 23 24 25 10 9 8 7 6 5 4 3 2
002–322793–Aug/2021

 The Metropolitan Museum of Art
New York

ISBN 978-0-7440-3362-5

DK books are available at special discounts when purchased in bulk for sales
promotions, premiums, fund-raising, or educational use. For details, contact:
DK Publishing Special Markets,
1450 Broadway, Suite 801, New York, NY 10018
SpecialSales@dk.com

Printed and bound in China

Acknowledgments
DK would like to thank Lisa Silverman Meyers, Laura Barth, Leanne
Graeff, Emily Blumenthal, Morgan Pearce, and all the curators
at The Met; Hilary Becker; Julie Ferris and Lisa Lanzarini;
Megan Douglass; Aaron Cushley; and Will Mabbitt.

For the curious

www.dk.com
www.metmuseum.org